THE HIPPO BOOK OF HILARIOUS POETRY

COMPILED BY TERRY DEARY

Illustrated by Stuart Trotter

Hippo Books
Scholastic Publications Limited
London

Scholastic Publications Ltd,
10 Earlham Street, London WC2H 9RX, UK

Scholastic Inc,
730 Broadway, New York, NY 10003, USA

Scholastic Tab Publications Ltd,
123 Newkirk Road, Richmond Hill,
Ontario L4C 3G5, Canada

Ashton Scholastic Pty Ltd,
P O Box 579, Gosford, New South Wales,
Australia

Ashton Scholastic Ltd,
165 Marua Road, Panmure, Auckland 6,
New Zealand

This collection first published by Scholastic Publications
Limited, 1989

ISBN 0 590 76131 5

Made and printed by Cox & Wyman Ltd, Reading, Berks
Typeset by AKM Associates (UK) Ltd, Southall, Middx.

10 9 8 7 6 5 4 3 2 1

ACKNOWLEDGEMENTS

The Compilers and Publishers of this collection would like to thank the following for granting permission to reproduce copyright material:

A GOOD POEM by Roger McGough, copyright © R McGough and reproduced from *In the Glassroom* published by Jonathan Cape Ltd; DADDY FELL INTO THE POND by Alfred Noyes, © A Noyes reproduced from *Alfred Noyes: Collected Poems* published by John Murray (Publishers) Ltd; COME ON IN THE WATER'S LOVELY by Gareth Owen, copyright © G Owen and reproduced from *Song of the City* published by Collins Publishers; GAMES by John Price, © J Price; BOOTERIES AND FLUTERIES by N M Bodecker, copyright © N M Bodecker reproduced from *Let's Marry Said the Cherry* published by Faber and Faber Ltd; I'M JUST GOING OUT FOR A MOMENT by Michael Rosen, copyright © M Rosen reproduced from *Wouldn't You Like to Know* published by André Deutsch Ltd; THE VULTURE, HENRY KING and THE FROG by Hilaire Belloc, copyright © H Belloc reproduced from *Complete Verse* by kind permission of Gerald Duckworth & Co Ltd; THE GLUTTON, NELLY NILLIS and ODE TO MY MOTHER reproduced from *Unspun Socks*, published by Michael Joseph Ltd in association with M & J Hobbs, and GRANNY from *Silly Verse for Kids* by Spike Milligan, copyright © Spike Milligan; NIGHT-STARVATION OR THE BITER BIT by Carey Blyton, copyright © C Blyton reproduced from *Bananas in Pyjamas* published by Faber and Faber Ltd; OH I WISH I'D LOOKED AFTER ME TEETH, IN DEFENCE OF HEDGEHOGS and LIKE YOU WOULD by Pam Ayres, copyright © P Ayres; THE BODYSNATCHER'S SONG by Tony Davies, copyright © Tony Davies; HISTORY OF A KNOW-ALL by Joanne Fowdy, copyright © J Fowdy; THE HIPPOCRUMP reproduced from *James Reeves: The Complete Poems for Children* and MR TOM NARROW reproduced from *The Wandering Moon and Other Poems* by James Reeves, copyright © J Reeves and reprinted by kind permission of The James Reeves Estate; I USED TO KEEP A BLUE MACAW by Roger McGough, copyright © R McGough and reproduced from *An Imaginary Menagerie* published by Viking Kestrel; COLONEL FAZACKERLEY by Charles Causley, copyright © C Causley reproduced from *Figgie Hobbin* published by Macmillan Publishers Ltd; THE VAMPIRE SAID by Max Fatchen, copyright © M Fatchen and reproduced from *Petrifying Poems* published by Omnibus Books, Australia; HUNTER TRIALS by John Betjeman, copyright © J Betjeman and reproduced from *John Betjeman's Collected Verse* published by John Murray (Publishers) Ltd; PUDDIN' SONG by Norman Lindsay, copyright © Janet Glad 1918 and reproduced from *The Magic Pudding* published by Angus & Robertson (UK); SERGEANT BROWN'S PARROT by Kit Wright, copyright © K Wright and reproduced from *Rabbiting On* published by Collins Publishers (UK);

CONTENTS

That's Funny

A Good Poem

I like a good poem
one with lots of fighting
in it. Blood, and the
clanging of armour. Poems

against Scotland are good,
and poems that defeat
the French with crossbows.
I don't like poems that

aren't about anything.
Sonnets are wet and
a waste of time.
Also poems that don't

know how to rhyme.
If I was a poem
I'd play football and
get picked for England.

Roger McGough

Daddy Fell Into the Pond

Everyone grumbled. The sky was grey.
We had nothing to do and nothing to say.
We were nearing the end of a dismal day.
And there seemed to be nothing beyond.
   Then
      Daddy fell into the pond!

And everyone's face grew merry and bright,
And Timothy danced for sheer delight.
'Give me the camera, quick, oh quick!
He's crawling out of the duckweed!' Click!

Then the gardener suddenly slapped his knee,
And doubled up, shaking silently,
And the ducks all quacked as if they were daft,
And it sounded as if the old drake laughed.
Oh, there wasn't a thing that didn't respond
   When
      Daddy fell into the pond!

Alfred Noyes

Don't Jump Off the Roof, Dad!

Don't jump off the roof, dad,
You'll make a hole in the yard!
Mum's just planted petunias,
The weeding and seeding was hard.

If you must end it all, dad,
Won't you please give us a break?
Just take a walk in the park, dad . . .
And then you can jump in the lake!

Anon

Come on in the Water's Lovely

Come on in the water's lovely
It isn't really cold at all
Of course you'll be quite safe up this end
If you hold tight to the wall.

Of course that fat boy there won't drown you
He's too busy drowning Gail
Just imagine you're a tadpole.
I *know* you haven't got a tail.

Oh come on in the water's lovely
Warm and clear as anything
All the bottom tiles are squiggly
And your legs like wriggly string.

Come on in the water's lovely
It's no good freezing on the side
How do you know you're going to drown
Unless you've really tried.

What? You're really going to do it?
You'll jump in on the count of three?
Of course the chlorine doesn't blind you
Dive straight in and you'll soon see.

One – it isn't really deep at all.
Two – see just comes to my chin.
Three – oh there's the bell for closing time
And just as you jumped in!

Gareth Owen

Games

I hate games
When the cold November wind
Freezes your knees,
White and knocking,
And the mud squirts
Up your shorts
When some fat show-off
Flattens you in rugby.

Or they make you
Struggle up treadmill hills
In something called cross-country,
But which is really
Cross slag-heap
(Made into a park
Now used as a dogs toilet.)
And even rain
Brings no release:
It's into the dusty sports hall
Chasing a huge orange basketball
You never touch
And being bumped and battered
In a no-contact game
(The teacher says.)
On such days
The happiest sound
Is the drawn out squeal
Of the final whistle.

John Price

Booteries and Fluteries and Flatteries and Things

If a place where they sell boots is called
a bootery,
then a place where they sell flutes must be
a flutery.
A place where they sell fish must be
a fishery,
and a china seller's shop
a cup'n'dishery.
A house that's full of flats is quite
a flattery,
but one that's full of bats is just
a battery.
A place to get your pots in is
a pottery,
but if you need a lot, you need
a lottery.
Some hospitals get nurses in a
nursery,
some pursers get their purses in
a pursery,
some people keep their grannies in
a granary
or send them for a tan to someone's
tannery.
The place to keep young misses is
a missery
(but if it's his not hers it's called
a hisery).
A safe place for Miss Greene is in
a greenery,
so if she makes a scene, she's in
a scenery.

For the crocodiles are watching from
the crockery
and the mocking birds are scowling in
the mockery,
and someone's sure to trick you in
the trickery,
to make you laugh and hiccup in
the hickory,
or make you spell forever in
the spellery,
in the deepest, darkest cellar in
the celery.
So you'd better do your sums now in
the summary
and afterward stay mum in someone's
mummery,
for the actors want to put you in their
actory,
and that's a fact, in anybody's
factory.

N Bodecker

Why English is so Hard

We'll begin with a box, and the plural is boxes;
But the plural of ox should be oxen, not oxes.
Then one fowl is goose, but two are geese;
Yet the plural of moose should never be meese.
You may find a lone mouse or a whole lot of
    mice,
But the plural of house is houses, not hice.
If the plural of man is always called men,
Why shouldn't the plural of pan be called pen?
The cow in the plural may be cows or kine.
But the plural of vow is vows, not vine.
And I speak of a foot, and you show me your
    feet,
But I give you a boot – would a pair be called
    beet?

If one is a tooth and a whole set are teeth,
Why shouldn't the plural of booth be called
    beeth?
If the singular is this, and the plural is these,
Should the plural of kiss be nicknamed kese?
Then one may be that, and three may be those,
Yet the plural of hat would never be hose.
We speak of a brother, and also of brethren,
But though we say mother, we never say
    methren.
The masculine pronouns are he, his, and him,
But imagine the feminine she, shis, and shim!
So our English, I think you will all agree,
Is the trickiest language you ever did see.

Unknown

I'm Just Going Out for a Moment

I'm just going out for a moment.
Why?
To make a cup of tea.
Why?
Because I'm thirsty.
Why?
Because it's hot.
Why?
Because the sun's shining.
Why?
Because it's summer.
Why?
Because that's when it is.
Why?
Why don't you stop saying why?
Why?
Tea-time why.
High-time-you-stopped-saying-why-time.
What?

Michael Rosen

Doctor Bell

Doctor Bell fell down the well
And broke his collar bone.
Doctors should attend the sick
And leave the well alone.

Anon

That's Horrible

Little Dog

Little dog
Crossing street.
Motor car . . .
Sausage meat.

Traditional

The Vulture

The vulture eats between his meals,
    And that's the reason why
He very, very rarely feels
    As well as you or I.

His eye is dull, his head is bald,
    His neck is growing thinner.
Oh! What a lesson for us all
    To only eat at dinner!

Hilaire Belloc

Green and Yellow

Where have you been all the day,
My boy Willie?
Where have you been all the day,
My own lovely son?

> In the woods, dear Mother,
> In the woods, dear Mother.
> Oh Mother be quick
> I wanna be sick
> And lay me down to die!

What did you do in them woods,
My boy Willie?
What did you do in them woods,
My own lovely one?

> I ate, dear Mother,
> I ate, dear Mother.
> Oh Mother be quick
> I wanna be sick
> And lay me down to die!

What did you eat in them woods,
My boy Willie?
What did you eat in them woods,
My own dearest one?

> Eels, dear Mother,
> Eels, dear Mother.
> Oh Mother be quick
> I wanna be sick
> And lay me down to die!

What colour was them eels my son,
My boy Willie?
What colour was them eels my son,
My own currant bun?

> Green and yeller,
> Green and yeller.
> Oh Mother be quick
> I wanna be sick
> And lay me down to die!

Them wasn't eels them was snakes my son,
My boy Willie,
Them wasn't eels them was snakes my son,
My own lovely one.

Yeuchchch! dear Mother,
Yeuchchch! dear Mother,
Oh Mother be quick
I wanna be sick
And lay me down to die!

What colour flowers would you like on your
    grave,
My boy Willie?
What colour flowers would you like on your
    grave,
My own dearest son?

Green and yeller!
Green and yeller!
Oh Mother be quick
I wanna be sick
And lay me down to d
                    i
                  e
                    !

Traditional

18

My Baby Has Gone Down the Plughole!

A mother was bathing her baby one night,
The youngest of ten and a terrible sight.
The mother was poor and the baby was thin,
'Twas nought but a skellington covered in skin.

The mother turned round for the soap from the
     rack,
She was only a moment, but when she turned
     back . . .
'My baby has gawn!' in anguish she cried.
'Oh, where is my baby?' the angels replied . . .

'Your baby has gawn down the plughole,
Your baby has gawn down the plug.
The poor little mite was so skinny and thin,
He should have been washed in a jug (or a tin!).

'Your baby is perfectly happy
And much better off than before.
He's a-mucking about with the angels above,
Not lost but gawn before!'

Traditional

The Glutton

Oh Molly, Molly, Molly
I've eaten too much pie
I've eaten too much custard
I think I'm going to die!

Just one more plate of jelly
Before I pass away
Another glass of lemonade
And then no more I say!

Perhaps just one banana
And one more lollipop
A little slice of Eccles cake
And then I'll *have* to stop!

So now one more one more goodbye!
and one more slice of ham
and now goodbye forever
But first some bread and jam.

So now I die, goodbye again
But pass the Stilton cheese
And as I slowly pass away
Just one more dinner please.

Spike Milligan

An Old Man of Blackheath

There was an old man of Blackheath
Who sat on his set of false teeth.
    Said he with a start,
      'Oh Lord, bless my heart!
I've bitten myself underneath!'

Anon

Night-starvation or The Biter Bit

At night, my Uncle Rufus
(Or so I've heard it said)
Would put his teeth into a glass
Of water by his bed.

At three o'clock one morning
He woke up with a cough,
And as he reached out for his teeth –
They bit his hand right off.

Carey Blyton

Henry King

The chief defect of Henry King
  Was chewing little bits of string;
At last he swallowed some which tied
  Itself in ugly Knots inside.

Physicians of the Utmost Fame
  Were called at once; but when they came
They answered, as they took their Fees,
  'There is no Cure for this Disease.

'Henry will very soon be dead.'
  His Parents stood about his bed
Lamenting his Untimely Death,
  When Henry, with his Latest Breath,

Cried, 'Oh, my Friends, be warned by me,
  That Breakfast, Dinner, Lunch and Tea,
Are all the Human Frame requires . . .'
  With that, the Wretched Child expires.

Hilaire Belloc

Oh, I Wish I'd Looked After me Teeth

Oh, I wish I'd looked after me teeth,
And spotted the perils beneath,
All the toffees I chewed,
And the sweet sticky food,
Oh, I wish I'd looked after me teeth.

I wish I'd been that much more willin'
When I had more tooth there than fillin'
To pass up gobstoppers,
From respect to me choppers,
And to buy something else with me shillin'.

When I think of the lollies I licked,
And the liquorice allsorts I picked,
Sherbet dabs, big and little,
All that hard peanut brittle,
My conscience gets horribly pricked.

My mother, she told me no end,
'If you got a tooth, you got a friend'.
I was young then, and careless,
My toothbrush was hairless,
I never had much time to spend.

Oh I showed them the toothpaste all right,
I flashed it about late at night,
But up-and-down brushin'
And pokin' and fussin'
Didn't seem worth the time – I could bite!

If I'd known I was paving the way
To cavities, caps and decay,
The murder of fillin's
Injections and drillin's,
I'd have thrown all me sherbet away.

So I lay in the old dentist's chair,
And I gaze up his nose in despair,
And his drill it do whine,
In these molars of mine,
'Two amalgum,' he'll say, 'for in there.'

How I laughed at my mother's false teeth,
As they foamed in the waters beneath.
But now comes the reckonin'
It's *me* they are beckonin'
Oh, I *wish* I'd looked after me teeth.

Pam Ayres

The Bodysnatcher's Song

When your granny kicks the bucket in her bed,
Let the poor old lady rest her tired head.
When your granny is deceased, just let her rest
    in peace
And don't dig up your granny when she's dead.

I tried to sell my Granny for a profit;
I thought I'd buy a load of food and scoff it.
I should have used my head; I should have
    stayed in bed,
Cos did I make a profit? Oh, come off it!

I went into the churchyard, I felt bold.
The tombstones told of victims young and old.
I thought I'd make five pounds, for some
    digging in the grounds,
But all I ever got there was a cold.

I had the chance of riches, but I blew it.
I never get the breaks – I should have knew it.
My Mum and Dad were smart – they'd got six
    hours start;
The rotten greedy turnips beat me to it!

So sell your Auntie Liz or Uncle Ned,
It'll serve them right for the wicked life they've
    led.
But when Granny's six foot deep, let her have
    her well-earned sleep,
And don't dig up your granny when she's dead.

When your granny kicks the bucket in her bed,
Let the poor old lady rest her tired head.
When your granny is deceased, just let her rest
    in peace,
And don't dig up your granny when she's dead.

Tony Davies

That's Incredible

Nickety Nurphy

There was a man in our back lane
Sold kippers for three ha'pence.
He sold me,
He sold me,
He sold me twenty four.

At first I would not buy them,
But after thinking twice,
I bought them for three ha'pence
And gave them to my wife.

So all day long she bent her mind
to matters of a phoney kind,
and finally, young Suzy said
(And proudly, too!) 'The sky is red!'

Knowing her mistake was past
she, happy and relaxed, fell fast
asleep – but in the black of night
a straying iron meteorite
got all burnt up to ashy dust
and stained the stratosphere with rust.
So when poor Suzy left her bed
next day – Alas! The sky was red!
And people said: 'The truth is out –
that girl is *always right*, no doubt!'

So Suzy tried to make abatement
by spouting quite the daftest statement.
She said: 'Our garden birds can't fly!'
(She hadn't noticed passing by,
A van with penguins from the zoo
had broken down, with doors askew,
and dozens of the flightless creatures
were eating grandmother's prize freesias.)
So poor old Suzy's plan had failed;
What could she do? she wailed and wailed.
She summoned every ounce courageous,
saying something quite outrageous.
'I', she thought, 'will tell them that
I think it's true the world is flat!'

It was across the headlines plastered,
and everyone was flabbergasted.
But Suzy was so much relieved,
that rubbish couldn't be believed!
She needn't worry any longer
about the threat of being wrong.
A feeling like a royal pardon
sent her, free, into the garden.
But, just beyond the privet hedge,
she discovered the end of the world
and fell off the e
                    d
                      g
                        e
                          !

Joanne Fowdy

Nelly Ninnis

There was a young girl called Nelly
Who had a nylon belly
The skin was so thin
We could all see in
It was full of Custard and Jelly

*By Jane and dad on way back
from Natural History Museum
15 Oct. 1977*

Jane and Spike Milligan

33

The Hippocrump

Along the valley of the Ump
Gallops the fearful Hippocrump.
His hide is leathery and thick;
His eyelids open with a *Click!*
His mouth he closes with a *Clack!*
He has three humps upon his back;
On each of these there grows a score
Of horny spikes, and sometimes more.
His hair is curly, thick and brown;
Beneath his chin a beard hangs down.
He has eight feet with hideous claws;
His nick is long – and O his jaws!
The boldest falters in his track
To hear those hundred teeth go *Clack!*

The Hippocrump is fierce indeed,
But if he eats the baneful weed
That grows beside the Purple Lake,
His hundred teeth begin to ache.
Then how the creature stamps and roars
Along the Ump's resounding shores!
The drowsy cattle faint with fright;
The birds fall flat, the fish turn white.
Even the rocks begin to shake;
The children in their beds awake;
The old ones quiver, quail, and quake.
'Alas!' they cry. 'Make no mistake,
It is *Himself* – he's got the Ache
From eating by the Purple Lake!'
Some say, 'It is *Old You-know-who* –
He's in a rage: what *shall* we do?'

'Lock up the barns, protect the stores,
Bring all the pigs and sheep indoors!'
They call upon their god, Agw-ump
To save them from the Hippocrump.
'What's that I hear go hop-skip-jump?
He's coming! Stand aside there!' *Bump!*
Lump-lump! – 'He's on the bridge now!' – *Lump!*
'I hear his tail' – *ker-flump, ker-flump!*
'I see the prickles on his hump!
It *is*, it IS – 'the Hippocrump!
Defend us now, O Great Agw-ump!'

Thus prayed the dwellers by the Ump.
Their prayer was heard. A broken stump
Caught the intruder in the rump.
He slipped into the foaming river,
Whose icy water quenched his fever,
Then while the creature floundering lay,
The timid people ran away;
And when the morrow dawned serene
The Hippocrump was no more seen.
Glad hymns of joy the people raised:
'For ever Great Agw-ump be praised!'

James Reeves

Colonel Fazackerley

Colonel Fazackerley Butterworth-Toast
Bought an old castle complete with a ghost,
But someone or other forgot to declare
To Colonel Fazack that the spectre was there.

On the very first evening, while waiting to dine,
The Colonel was taking a fine sherry wine,
When the ghost, with a furious flash and a flare,
Shot out of the chimney and shivered, 'Beware!'

Colonel Fazackerley put down his glass
And said, 'My dear fellow, that's really first
        class!
I just can't conceive how you do it at all.
I imagine you're going to a Fancy Dress Ball?'

At this, the dread ghost gave a withering cry.
Said the Colonel (his monocle firm in his eye),
'Now just how you do it I wish I could think.
Do sit down and tell me, and please have a
        drink.'

The ghost in his phosphorous cloak gave a roar
And floated about between ceiling and floor.
He walked through a wall and returned through
        a pane
And backed up the chimney and came down
        again.

Said the Colonel, 'With laughter I'm feeling
        quite weak!'
(As trickles of merriment ran down his cheek).
'My house-warming party I hope you won't
        spurn.
You *must* say you'll come and you'll give us a
        turn!'

At this, the poor spectre – quite out of his wits –
Proceeded to shake himself almost to bits.
He rattled his chains and he clattered his bones
And he filled the whole castle with mumbles and
     moans.

But Colonel Fazackerley, just as before,
Was simply delighted and called out, 'Encore!'
At which the ghost vanished, his efforts in vain,
And never was seen in the castle again.

'Oh dear, what a pity!' said Colonel Fazack.
'I don't know his name, so I can't call him
     back.'
And then with a smile that was hard to define,
Colonel Fazackerley went in to dine.

Charles Causley

The Good Ship Calabah

Well come all you dry land sailors and listen to
    this song,
It's only a thousand verses, it won't detain you
    long,
Concerning the adventures of this old Lisburn
    barge,
When I sailed as man before the mast on the
    good ship Calabah.

The captain was a strapping man, he stood just
    four feet two,
His eyes were pink, his nose was green and his
    cheeks a shade of blue,
He wore a leather medal that he won in the
    Crimey War,
And the captain's wife was passenger cook on
    the good ship Calabah.

'Well look here young man,' the captain said,
    'look here young man,' says he,
'Would you like to be a sailor and sail the raging
    sea?

Would you like to be a sailor on foreign lands to
     roam?
For we're under orders for Ballantyre with half a
     ton of coal.'

Well three months after we set sail, sure the
     weather it was sublime,
As we passed beneath the railway bridge I heard
     the town clock chime,
And then we came to the gasworks straits, a very
     dangerous part,
And we ran aground on a lump of coal that
     wasn't marked up in the charts.
All became confusion and the raging winds did
     blow,
The bo's'n slipped on some orange peel and he
     fell to the hold below,
'Put on more speed,' the captain cried, 'you
     know we're sorely pressed.'
And the engineer from the bank replied, 'Sure
     the horse is doing his best!'

Then we all fell into the water and we all let out
     a roar.
An old farmer standing on the bank pulled me
     to the shore.
I'll go no more a sailing or brave the raging
     main,
Next time I go to Ballantyre, I'll take the
     blooming train.

Traditional

I Used to Keep a Blue Macaw

I used to keep
   a blue macaw
in my bedside
   bottom drawer

But he was never
happy there
among my socks
and underwear

He pined for sunshine
    trees galore
as in Brazil
    and Ecuador

Knowing then
    what I must do
I journeyed south
    as far as Kew

In the Gardens
    set him free
(wasn't that macaw-
    ful of me?)

Roger McGough

That's Silly

There Was a Man

There was a man, he went mad,
He jumped into a paper bag.

The paper bag was too narrow,
He jumped into a wheelbarrow.

The wheelbarrow ran away,
He jumped into a cart of hay.

The cart of hay caught on fire,
He jumped into a pig's byer.

The pig's byer was too nasty,
He jumped into an apple pasty.

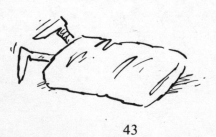

The apple pasty was too sweet,
He jumped into Chester le Street.

Chester le Street was full of stones,
He fell down and broke his bones.

Traditional

The Vampire Said

The vampire said: 'My name is mud
Because I have a taste for blood
And there are those who think I'm horrid
For nipping victims on the forehead.
But, on this matter I won't hedge.
What really sets my teeth on edge
And scares me even more than rabies
Are children biting jelly babies.'

Max Fatchen

Hunter Trials

It's awf'lly bad luck on Diana,
    Her ponies have swallowed their bits;
She fished down their throats with a spanner
    And frightened them all into fits.

So now she's attempting to borrow.
    Do lend her some bits, Mummy, do;
I'll lend her my own for tomorrow,
    But today, I'll be wanting them too.

Just look at Prunella on Guzzle,
    The wizardest pony on earth;
Why doesn't she slacken the muzzle
    And tighten the breech in his girth?

I say, Mummy, there's Mrs. Geyser
    And doesn't she look pretty sick?
I bet it's because Mona Lisa
    Was hit on the hock with a brick.

Miss Blewitt says Monica threw it,
    But Monica says it was Joan
And Joan's very thick with Miss Blewitt,
    So Monica's sulking alone.

And Margaret failed in her paces,
    Her withers got tied in a noose,
So her coronets caught in the traces
    And now all her fetlocks are loose.

Oh, it's me now. I'm terribly nervous.
    I wonder if Smudges will shy.
She's practically certain to swerve as
    Her Pelham is over one eye.

Oh wasn't it naughty of Smudges?
  Oh, Mummy, I'm sick with disgust,
She threw me in front of the Judges,
  And my silly old collarbone's bust.

John Betjeman

She Stood on the Bridge at Midnight

She stood on the bridge at midnight,
Her heart was all a-quiver.
She gave a cough, her leg fell off,
And floated down the river.

Anon

Puddin' Song

Oh, who would be a puddin',
   A puddin' in a pot,
A puddin' which is stood on
   A fire which is hot?
Oh sad indeed the lot
Of puddin's in a pot.

I wouldn't be a puddin'
   If I could be a bird,
If I could be a wooden
   Doll, I would'n' say a word.
Yes, I have often heard
It's grand to be a bird.

But as I am a puddin',
   A puddin' in a pot,
I hope you get the stomachache
   For eatin' me a lot.
I hope you get it hot,
You puddin'-eatin' lot!

Norman Lindsay

The Frog

Be kind and tender to the Frog,
   And do not call him names,
As 'Slimy skin', or 'Polly-wog',
   Or likewise 'Ugly James',
Or 'Gap-a-grin', or 'Toad-gone-wrong',
   Or 'Billy Bandy-knees':
The Frog is justly sensitive
   To epithets like these.
No animal will more repay
   A treatment kind and fair;
At least so lonely people say
Who keep a frog (and, by the way,
They are extremely rare).

Hilaire Belloc

A Tutor who Taught on the Flute

A tutor who taught on the flute
Tried to teach two young tutors to toot.
Said the two to the tutor
'Is it harder to toot, or
To tutor two tooters to toot?'

Anon

John Bun

Here lies John Bun,
He was killed by a gun,
His name was not Bun, but Wood,
But Wood would not rhyme with gun, but
Bun would.

Anon

Sergeant Brown's Parrot

Many policemen wear upon their shoulders
cunning little radios. To pass away the time
They talk about the traffic to them, listen to the
    news,
And it helps them to Keep Down Crime.

But Sergeant Brown, he wears upon his shoulder
A tall green parrot as he's walking up and down
And all the parrot says is 'Who's a-pretty-
    boy-then?'
'I am,' says Sergeant Brown.

Kit Wright

Ode to my Mother

If I should die,
Think only this of me,
The swine left owing us
Six pounds eighty p.

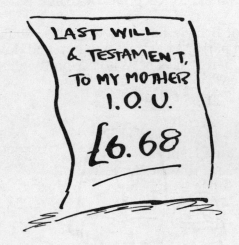

Spike Milligan

That's Nasty

Patience

When ski-ing in the Engadine
My hat blew off down a ravine.
My son, who went to fetch it back,
Slipped through an icy glacier's crack,
And then got permanently stuck.
It really was infernal luck;
My hat was practically new
I loved my little Henry too
And I may have to wait for years
Till either of them reappears.

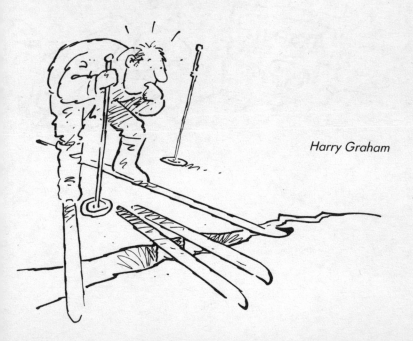

Harry Graham

Notting Hill Polka

We've – had –
A Body in the house
    Since Father passed away;
He took bad on
Saturday night an' he
    Went the followin' day.

Mum's – pulled –
The blinds all down
    An' bought some Sherry Wine,
An' we've put the tin
What the Arsenic's in
    At the bottom of the Ser-pen-tine!

W Bridges-Adams

Piano Practice

A doting father once there was
Who loved his daughter Gerda,
Until she got the piano craze –
Then how the passion stirred her!
Her fingers were wild elephants' feet,
And as month after month he heard her.
He tried every way
To stop her play
From bribery to murder.

One day when she was practising,
He popped up behind and caught her
And dumped her in his wheelbarrow
And carried her off to slaughter.

Tipping her into a well, he cried,
'Hurrah! I've drowned my daughter!'
But a voice from the well
Rang out like a bell,
'Aha – there isn't any water!'

Ian Serraillier

Granny

Through every nook and every cranny
The wind blew in on poor old Granny;
Around her knees, into each ear
(And up her nose as well, I fear).

All through the night the wind grew worse,
It nearly made the vicar curse.
The top had fallen off the steeple
Just missing him (and other people).

It blew on man; it blew on beast.
It blew on nun; it blew on priest.
It blew the wig off Auntie Fanny –
But most of all, it blew on Granny!

Spike Milligan

Quiet Fun

My son Augustus, in the street, one day,
Was feeling quite exceptionally merry.
A stranger asked him: 'Can you show me, pray,
The quickest way to Brompton Cemetery?'
'The quickest way? You bet I can!' says Gus.
And pushed the fellow underneath a bus.

Whatever people say about my son,
He does enjoy his little bit of fun.

Harry Graham

In Defence of Hedgehogs

I am very fond of hedgehogs
Which makes me want to say,
That I am struck with wonder,
How there's any left today,
For each morning as I travel
And no short distance that,
All I see are hedgehogs,
Squashed. And dead. And flat.

Now. Hedgehogs are not clever,
No. Hedgehogs are quite dim,
And when he sees your headlamps,
Well, it don't occur to him,
That the very wisest thing to do
Is up and run away,
No! he curls up in a stupid ball,
And no doubt starts to pray.

Well, motor cars do travel
At a most alarming rate,
And by the time you sees him,
It is very much too late,
And thus he gets a-squasho'd,
Unrecorded but for me,
With me pen and paper,
Sittin' in a tree.

It is statistically proven,
In chapter and in verse,
That in a car and hedgehog fight,
The hedgehog comes off worse.
When whistlin' down your prop shaft,
And bouncin' off your diff,
His coat of nice brown prickles,
Is not effect-iff.

A hedgehog cannot make you laugh,
Whistle, dance or sing,
And he ain't much to look at,
And he don't make anything,
And in amongst his prickles,
There's fleas and bugs and that,
But there ain't no need to leave him,
Squashed. And dead. And flat.

Oh spare a thought for hedgehogs,
Spare a thought for me.
Spare a thought for hedgehogs,
As you drink your cup of tea,
Spare a thought for hedgehogs,
Hoverin' on the brinkt,
Spare a thought for hedgehogs,
Lest they become extinct.

Pam Ayres

The Crocodile

No animal is half so vile
As Crocky-Wock the crocodile.
On Saturdays he likes to crunch
Six juicy children for his lunch,
And he especially enjoys
Just three of each, three girls, three boys.
He smears the boys (to make them hot)
With mustard from the mustard pot.
But mustard doesn't go with girls,
It tastes all wrong with plaits and curls.
With them, what goes extremely well
Is butterscotch and caramel.
It's such a super marvellous treat
When boys are hot and girls are sweet.
At least that's Crocky's point of view.
He ought to know. He's had a few.
That's all for now. It's time for bed
Lie down and rest your sleepy head . . .

Ssh! *Listen*! What is that I hear
Gallumphing softly up the stair?
Go lock the door and fetch my gun!
Go on, child, hurry! Quickly, run!
No, stop! Stand back! He's coming in!
Oh look, that greasy greenish skin!
The shining teeth, the greedy smile!
It's CROCKY-WOCK, THE CROCODILE!

Roald Dahl

School Dinners

If you stay to school dinners,
Better throw them aside;
A lot of kids didn't and
A lot of kids died.

The meat is made of iron,
The spuds are made of steel,
And if that don't get yer,
The afters will.

Anon

Mr Tom Narrow

A scandalous man
Was Mr Tom Narrow,
He pushed his grandmother
Round in a barrow.
And he called out loud
As he rang his bell,
'Grannies to sell!
Old grannies to sell!'

The neighbours said,
As they heard his cry
'This poor old lady
We will not buy.
He surely must be
A mischievous man
To try for to sell
His own dear Gran.'
'Besides,' said another,
'If you ask me,
She'd be very small use
That I can see.'
'You're right,' said a third,
'And no mistake –
A very poor bargain
She'd surely make.'

So Mr Tom Narrow
He scratched his head,
And he sent his grandmother
Back to bed;
And he rang his bell
Through all the town
Till he sold his barrow
For half a crown.

James Reeves

If You Should Meet a Crocodile

If you should meet a crocodile
Don't take a stick and poke him;
Ignore the welcome in his smile,
Be careful not to stroke him.

For as he sleeps upon the Nile,
He thinner gets and thinner;
And whene'er you meet a crocodile
He's ready for his dinner.

Anon

That's Rude

The Boy Stood on the Burning Deck

The boy stood on the burning deck
    Picking his nose like mad.
He rolled them into little balls
    And flicked them at his dad.

Anon

The Boy Stood on the Burning Deck (again)

The boy stood on the burning deck,
His feet were full of blisters;
The flames came up and burned his pants,
And now he wears his sister's.

Anon

Oh Larty Tiddle

Oh larty tiddle what a cold I've got!
Getting out of bed and sitting on the pot.
The pot was cold,
Me bot was hot,
Oh larty tiddle what a cold I've got!

Anon

The Cowboy's Shame

The name of Frank Carew Macgraw
Was notorious in the West,
Not as the fastest on the draw
But cause he only wore a vest.

Yes just a vest and nothing more!
Through the Wild and Woolly West,
They knew the name of Frank Macgraw
Cause he only wore a vest.

Oh! His nether parts swung wild and free
As on his horse he sat.
He wore a vest and nothing else –
Oh! except a cowboy hat.

Yes! naked from the waist he rode –
He did not give two hoots!
Frank Macgraw in hat and vest
Oh! and a pair of boots.

But nothing else – no! not a stitch!
As through the cactus he
Rode on his horse, although of course
He did protect his knee.

With leather leggings – but that's all!
No wonder that his name
Was infamous throughout the West
And spoken of with shame.

Actually he *did* wear pants
On Sunday, and it's true
He also wore them other days –
And sometimes he wore two!

And often in an overcoat
You'd see him riding by,
But as he went men shook their heads
And ladies winked their eye,

For *everyone* knew Frank Macgraw
Throughout the Old Wild West –
Not because he broke the law
But cause he *only* wore a vest!

Terry Jones

Happy Birthday

Happy Birthday to you,
You live in a zoo.
You look like a monkey
And you act like one too!

Traditional

My Boyfriend Gave me an Apple

My boyfriend gave me an apple
My boyfriend gave me a pear
My boyfriend gave me a kiss on the lips
So I kicked him down the stairs.

I kicked him over Sunderland
I kicked him over France
I kicked him over Blackpool Tower
And he lost his underpants.

Anon

Tell-Tale Tit

Tell-tale tit
Your knickers will split,
Your dad's in the dustbin
Eating fish and chips.

Children's playground rhyme

Like You Would

Well I got up in the morning,
Like you would.
And I cooked a bit of breakfast,
Like you would,
But at the door I stopped,
For a message had been dropped,
And I picked it up, and read it,
Like you would.

'Oh Blimey!' I said,
Like you would,
'Have a read of this,
This is good!'
It said: 'I live across the way,
And admire you every day,
And my heart, it breaks without you.'
Well, it would.

It said: 'I'd buy you furs and jewels,
If I could.'
And I go along with that,
I think he should.
It said: 'Meet me in the Park,
When it's good and dark,
And so me wife won't see,
I'll wear a hood.'

Oh, I blushed with shame and horror,
Like you would,
That a man would ask me that,
As if I could!
So I wrote him back a letter,
Saying 'No, I think it's better,
If I meet you in the Rose and Crown,
Like we did last Thursday.'

Pam Ayres

Old Mother Hubbard's Mad Dog

Old Mother Hubbard
Went to the cupboard
To get her mad doggy a plum.
When she got there
The cupboard was bare
So the dog took a bite from her bum!

Anon

That's Ridiculous

Fine October Morning

It was a fine October morning,
In April, last July;
The sun lay thick upon the ground,
The snow shone in the sky.
Flowers were sweetly singing,
The birds were in full bloom;
I went downstairs to the cellar,
To sweep the upstairs room.

The time was Tuesday morning
On Wednesday, just at night;
I saw ten thousand miles away
A house just out of sight.
The doors they stuck out inwards,
The front was at the back;
It stood alone between two others,
And it was whitewashed black.

Anon

The Headless Gardener

A gardener, Tobias Baird,
Sent his head to be repaired;
He thought, as nothing much was wrong,
He wouldn't be without it long.

Ten years he's weeded path and plot,
A headless gardener, God wot,
Always hoping (hope is vain)
To see his noddle back again.

Don't pity him for his distress –
He never sent up his address.

Ian Serraillier

I Have Never Been So Happy

I have never been so happy
  Since my dear old Mom and Pappy
Packed the car and left real snappy
Said they'd had enough.

I can eat just what I feel like,
  Make up any kind of meal, like
Mars bars, chips and jellied eels, like
Mommy never made.

To nursery school I gave up going,
  They teach you nothing that's worth knowing,
And anyway there's movies showing
In the afternoons.

And bedtime, well, it's up to me now.
  Midnight, two or half past three now.
Sometimes I'll just watch TV now
All night long.

So if you're listening Mom and Pappy,
  As you can see I'm really happy,
But could you come, and change my nappy,
Mommy, Pappy, please!

Colin McNaughton

The Sloth

In moving-slow he has no Peer.
You ask him something in his ear,
He thinks about it for a Year;

And, then, before he says a Word
There, upside down (unlike a Bird),
He will assume that you have Heard –

A most Ex-as-per-at-ing Lug.
But should you call his manner Smug,
He'll sigh and give his Branch a Hug;

Then off again to Sleep he goes,
Still swaying gently by his Toes,
And you just *know* he knows he knows.

Theodore Roethke

There's an Awful Lot of Weirdos

There's an awful lot of weirdos
In our neighbourhood!
Yes, there's an awful lot of weirdos
In our neighbourhood!

I know this physical wreck,
Who has a bolt through his neck!
There's an awful lot of weirdos
In our neighbourhood.

And in an upstairs room,
An old lady rides a broom!
There's an awful lot of weirdos
In our neighbourhood.

A man lives on the square,
When he's in he isn't there!
There's an awful lot of weirdos
In our neighbourhood.

And that woman down the block,
Whose snaky hair's a shock!
There's an awful lot of weirdos
In our neighbourhood.

And someone near the dairy,
When the moon is out gets hairy!
There's an awful lot of weirdos
In our neighbourhood.

There's a guy who's green and scaly,
Has webbed feet and sells fish daily!
There's an awful lot of weirdos
In our neighbourhood.

We've a strange old feller,
With horns, down in the cellar!
There's an awful lot of weirdos
In our neighbourhood.

Think I'll leave this miscellanea,
And return to Transylvania,
'cause there's an awful lot of weirdos
In our neighbourhood.

Colin McNaughton

Tongue Twisters

Theophilus Thistledown

Theophilus Thistledown,
   the successful thistle sifter,
in sifting a sieve of unsifted thistles,
   Thrust three thousand thistles
through the thick of his thumb.
   If, then, Theophilus Thistledown,
the successful thistle sifter,
   thrust three thousand thistles
through the thick of his thumb,
   see that thou,
in sifting a sieve of thistles,
   do not get the unsifted thistles
stuck in *thy* thumb.

Anon

Ned Nott

Ned Nott was shot
 and Sam Shott was not.
So it is better to be Shott
 than Nott.
Some say Nott
 was not shot.
But Shott says
 he shot Nott.
Either the shot Shott shot at Nott
 was not shot,
 or
 Nott was shot.
If the shot Shott shot shot Nott,
 Nott was shot.
But if the shot Shott shot shot Shott,
 then Shott was shot
 not Nott.
However,
 the shot Shott shot shot not Shott –
 but Nott.

Betty Botter

Betty Botter
  bought some butter,
But, she said,
  the butter's bitter.
If I put it
  in my batter,
It will make
  my batter bitter.
But a bit
  of better butter –
That would make
  my batter better.
So she bought
  a bit of butter,
Better than
  her bitter butter.
And she put it
  in her batter,
And the batter
  was not bitter.
So 'twas better
  Betty Botter
Bought a bit
  of better butter.

Anon

Upside Down

It's funny how beetles
and creatures like that
can walk upside down
as well as walk flat:

They crawl on a ceiling
and climb on a wall
without any practice
or trouble at all,

While I have been trying
for a year (maybe more)
and still I can't stand
with my head on the floor.

Aileen Fisher

I've Lost my Car!

'I've lost my car, I've lost my car,
It's nowhere to be seen!
I've lost my car, I've lost my car,
And it was red and green!'

'I've found your car, I've found your car,
Outside the barber's shop!
I've found your car, I've found your car,
I am a clever cop!'

'A clever cop? Don't make me laugh,
You've no brains in your head!
The car I lost was red and green,
That car is green and red!'

Colin West

In the Bath

As I lay in the bath
        Tonight
I thank the Lord
        I'm water-tight.

Anon

Poetry

Roses are Red
Violets are Blue,
Most poems Rhyme
But this one doesn't.

Anon

Index of Titles

Index of Poets